# FINDING YOUR DESTINY

Follow your dreams &
always stay on purpose!

# FINDING
# YOUR
# DESTINY

*ACHIEVE YOUR DREAMS...*
## DREAM BIG!

## JOHN BRINSMEAD

**Disclaimer**
Both Mirrormont Press and the author are not liable for the use or misuse of the principles contained in this book; this book is not a substitute for professional legal, financial, or psychological advice.

First Edition

Book cover design and interior composition by Bookcovers.com

Publisher's Cataloging-in-Publication
(Provided by Quality Books, Inc.)

Brinsmead, John.
    Finding your destiny : achieve your dreams : dream big! / John Brinsmead. -- 1st ed.
    p. cm.
    Includes index.
    ISBN 0-9740099-5-4

    1. Goal (Psychology) 2. Conduct of life.
    3. Self-realization. 4. Success.   I. Title.

BF505.G6B75 2004            158.1
                    QBI03-700268

# DEDICATION

To Diana, my high school sweetheart, companion, and wife for 35 wonderful years: your understanding, nourishing, and supporting love has been the most important inspiration in my life.

# ACKNOWLEDGEMENTS

I would like to thank all of the individuals who helped with the development and production of this book: Lisa and Mark Gaul, Vicky and Steve Francis, Alice and Paul Hegna, Bob and Andrea Moawad, Mike and Debby Akiyama, Kristi Aravena, Susan Blanchett, Sonja Dolson, Jeannette Sugai, Eric Allenbaugh, June Cotner, Rob Sandstrom, Allen D'Angelo, Kim Leonard, Christine Blank, and the staff at Archer-Elison.

Special thanks to my wife, Diana Brinsmead: she is the only one who knows all the time and work required to create it. Most of all, I want to thank God for providing me the wisdom to make this dream come true.

# *TABLE OF CONTENTS*

# INTRODUCTION

You are holding in your hands a book that can change your life. It literally guides you to find your destiny. This book contains success secrets of the wisest people who have ever lived. These secrets work as well today as they did in ancient times.

Some of the concepts covered include:
- How to become a happier, more successful person.
- How to take responsibility for your life.
- How to use self-assessment to determine what you want from life.
- How to use your talent to clearly define your life's purpose.
- How to set and reach goals.
- How life's universal laws can work for you.
- How to use the power of Spirit.
- How to program your subconscious mind.
- How to face and conquer fear.

Most people have not been taught, and do not know, these concepts. They fail to recognize that they have the power within themselves to change their lives. The universe operates in harmony with a foundation of laws. These laws will be explained, and you will be shown how they can work for you.

The concepts you are about to learn are very powerful. When they are applied properly, they will increase your self-confidence, prosperity, happiness, and peace of mind. You will be able to make life better for yourself, your family, and people around you.

This book contains the most concise, updated information on these subjects. Reread it often to renew your understanding of the principles. Retake the exercises from time to time to confirm that your wants are still the same.

You have the power to achieve greatness. You can obtain anything you want from life if you are willing to put forth the energy and effort. We are living in a time that allows everyone the freedom to choose what he or she wants to do or be. Never before in the history of the world has it been possible for so many people to exercise and achieve their choice. There are unlimited opportunities to achieve success.

*If one advances confidently in the direction of his dreams, and endeavors to live the life which he has imagined, he will meet with success unexpected in common hours.*
HENRY DAVID THOREAU (AMERICAN ESSAYIST 1817-1862)

# SUCCESS AND HAPPINESS

Success is making progress toward your goal, having the tenacity to stick with it and bring it to reality. Successful people see the outcome and know they have the power within to accomplish what they want. They are confident in their abilities. Success builds success. Success is learned!

Happiness is a belief in and love of one's self. It is personal satisfaction; a feeling that you are pleased with the way you are living life. Happiness comes from within. It is a mental attitude, a state of consciousness. Happiness is available to all; you create it. Happiness is learned!

Many people have brief encounters with happiness. They view success and happiness as something that is acquired. Material wealth does not determine whether you are happy or not. Happiness cannot be purchased.

> *Happiness is the meaning and the purpose of life, the whole aim and end of human existence.*
> ARISTOTLE (GREEK PHILOSOPHER 384-322 BC)

## *Principles Of Happiness*

- *LIVE A VIRTUOUS LIFE*
Happiness is experienced when you live a virtuous life. Maintain high integrity. Never compromise your values or do anything that will make you think less of yourself.

- *YOU ARE THE CO-CREATOR OF YOUR LIFE*
Build a relationship with God and follow the guidance from within. Trust your inner wisdom: it is watchful of your best interests and will keep you on course. When you are in harmony with this power, you will find that your life flows and you feel at peace.

- *MAINTAIN A POSITIVE MENTAL ATTITUDE*
Focus your thoughts on all that is good, and happiness will come to you. Keep your thoughts positive, and refrain from complaining, belittling, and demeaning talk. Negative thoughts bring negative events into your life.

- *LIVE YOUR LIFE ON PURPOSE*
Happiness will occur when you find your life's purpose and use your God-given talent to fulfill it. Work steadily toward the achievement of your goals.

- *LOVE LIFE*
Take time to have fun. Love and enjoy life. Do the things that make you happy.

- *SERVE OTHERS*
Happiness is experienced when you serve others. Be generous. Give time and money to people in need. Altruism and generosity are part of human nature.

> *Success is getting what you want. Happiness is wanting what you get.*
>     DALE CARNEGIE (AMERICAN AUTHOR 1888-1955)

## Learn From The Past - Live In The Present

Learn from your past and start directing your life toward new goals and opportunities. You are the sum total of your past, present, and future. Have faith that your life will unfold as you have planned and live in the present. The present is the only time you are alive. You are free in the present moment. The present can consist of peace and contentment, if you allow your thoughts to be free of the past and future.

Many people are critical of their past behavior. They dwell on past mistakes, bringing these thoughts into the present. Past failures are gifts: learn from them to build your future. Never dwell on them! Resolve to correct future similar situations. Nothing is gained by dwelling on guilt, humiliation, shame, and embarrassment. Forgive yourself for making mistakes. Have high expectations as you move toward the future. Dwell on the kind of behavior you want in your life.

> *We live in the present, we dream of the future, and we learn eternal truths from the past.*
>     MME. CHIANG KAI-SHEK (CHINESE REVOLUTIONARY LEADER)

## Plan For Your Future

There are people who fear the future and worry about things to come. Have faith in your abilities and anticipate the future with high expectations. Always look forward. Know where you are going. The opportunities are in the future.

To experience happiness, determine where your current path is taking you. Project your thoughts forward from this point to the road you wish to travel. Discipline yourself to achieve the things you desire. Keep your thoughts toward the future.

> *I like the dreams of the future better than the history of the past.*
> THOMAS JEFFERSON
> (THIRD PRESIDENT OF THE UNITED STATES 1743-1826)

## Time Is Precious

Time is a precious commodity that should not be wasted. We are all given a finite amount of time to use however we want. Once used, it can never be retrieved, and it is not replaceable. Time is constantly being depleted and we cannot be sure how much of it we have left. We cannot check our balance. Live every day as if it were your last.

It is easy to get into a rut and live your life day after day, letting time slip away. People keep putting off doing the things they want to do, believing time is infinite. They think there is plenty of time to accomplish lifetime dreams and goals tomorrow. Before they know it, time has passed and, with it, their dreams and desires.

> *Dost thou love life? Then do not squander time, for that is the stuff life is made of.*
> BENJAMIN FRANKLIN (AMERICAN SCIENTIST, 1706-1790)

## One Life To Live

Are you fulfilling your wants and desires? Are you achieving your life's purpose? If your answer is "no", then ask yourself, "Why not?". Start spending time doing things that are important to you. Make it your highest priority to achieve daily progress towards your purpose and goals. Doing anything else is a waste of time and a waste of your life. Enjoy every minute you are here. Your life is not a rehearsal. You will not get a second chance at it. Make the most of it the first time around. Live each day to the fullest!

## *Summary*

- Happiness is experienced when you live with integrity and truth.
- Learn from your past, plan for the future, and enjoy the present.
- Determine why you are here and start working toward accomplishing your purpose.

# LOCUS OF CONTROL

Psychologists define locus of control as the perceived source of control over our behavior, viewed as being either internal or external. People with an internal locus of control take responsibility for their actions and view themselves as having control over their destiny. People with an external sense of control believe that control comes from outside forces. They think their success or failure depends on external events. An internal locus of control is essential to obtain what you want in life.

## Accepting Responsibility For Your Life
When you adopt the idea that you are responsible for where you are in your life, you are acknowledging that you are also responsible for your future. You have the power to choose, and, with this power, you can become anything you desire. Your choices, or failure to make choices, have created your life. You control your destiny!

Accept complete responsibility for your life. You are where you are right now because of the decisions you have made. You feel good about yourself to the degree in which you feel in control of your life. If you are happy, you have made wise decisions in the past. Alternatively, if you are unhappy, you likely have made unwise choices or postponed action on important issues. Research has shown that successful people control their lives. Successful people take responsibility for their actions. They constantly acknowledge that they are responsible for the events that occur in their lives.

Many people let outside circumstances and events direct their lives. They fail to have a clear sense of purpose and direction. They want everyone to do things for them and rarely rely on their own abilities. When things go wrong they blame others for the events instead of learning from their mistakes.

Full responsibility for your life can be a difficult concept to accept. There might be circumstances or events that have affected your life, in which you have had little or no control. You may not be responsible for the circumstances or events, but you are responsible for the way you react and respond to it. If you allow others to control you or you drift aimlessly going in circles without a sense of purpose, you chose this to occur.

Your perception of the source of control in your life is critical to your health and happiness. Become internally controlled and stay focused on what you want. Don't let circumstances and outside events direct your life. Deal with external events when they threaten you. Handle them the best you can, then return to your purpose. Always stay on purpose!

> *Man is responsible throughout every moment of his life for what*
> *he will make of the next hour, for how he will shape the next day.*
> VIKTOR FRANKL
> (AUSTRIAN PSYCHIATRIST/DEATH CAMP SURVIVOR 1905-1997)

## Change Is Possible

The good news is that you can change whatever is not working in your life. Within reason, you can achieve anything you desire and have anything you want. Usually, the biggest challenge is determining what you want out of life.

With the creative power of your mind, you can achieve anything. Determine what you want, set clear goals, and depend on your mind's higher abilities. The power to overcome any challenge is within you. This power will respond when you become self-reliant, depending on yourself to solve your problems. You can take control of your life, or you can let life control you.

> *The greatest discovery of any generation is that a human being can alter his life by altering his attitude of mind.*
> WILLIAM JAMES (AMERICAN PSYCHOLOGIST/PROFESSOR 1842-1910)

## Summary

- People with an external locus of control perceive control from outside forces. They blame others for circumstances and events that have altered their lives.
- People with an internal locus of control accept responsibility and take control of their lives. They do not let outside events direct their lives.
- An internal locus of control is essential for achieving health and happiness.
- You can change your life if you are not happy with it. You have the power to create your own destiny. Believe in your internal locus of control.

# SELF-DISCOVERY

The more you know about yourself, the more likely you are to recognize and achieve your full potential. You have unique interests, talents, and desires that define who you are, and what you view as meaningful. No one else on this earth has experienced your view of life. Raise your self-awareness, and you will discover your natural talents and wants. The better you understand your abilities, the better decisions you will make concerning your life and career.

Increase your self-awareness by answering the questions and exercises in this chapter. The answers will define your wants and desires. Review your answers and use them to contemplate and define your life's purpose. Finding your destiny is a spiritual experience. The answers are within. You are the only one who knows your life's purpose. You will need to get in touch with your true feelings to determine what you want from life.

Create a goal journal, or use the space provided in this book to record your answers. When you have run out of ideas, carry the list with you. Write down your thoughts as they come to you and record them in the journal. Keep in mind that it may take several months to answer the questions, and that your answers may change over time.

> *Know thyself.*
>
> INSCRIBED ON THE WALL OF THE TEMPLE OF APOLLO
> (4TH CENTURY B.C.)

## Values

A value is an individual standard or quality that you feel is worthwhile. Become aware and understand your values. Great personal satisfaction can be achieved when your values are aligned with your life's mission and goals. Know your values and follow them. This is the key to having peace of mind, happiness, and success. There will be times in your life when you will face difficult decisions. Use your values to guide you. Trust and follow the guidance of your spirit. There will also be times when you will be tempted to compromise your values. Never compromise them! Follow your values, regardless of the cost. You will experience satisfaction and confidence, knowing you have done the right thing. Live righteously, and follow Shakespeare's advice "To thine own self be true."

Values are different for different people. What are your values? What is important in your life? What values do you live by? Identify your values and prioritize them. This is harder than it sounds. You might find it helpful to write each of your values on a three by five card. Thoughtfully arrange them to determine their priority. You should end up with just a few high priority values. Prioritizing your values means that your number one value will take precedence over your number two value. When you are faced with a choice between value one and value two, you should always choose the top-rated value.

> *Live so that when your children think of fairness caring and integrity, they think of you.*
>
> H. JACKSON BROWNE, JR. (AMERICAN AUTHOR)

## VALUE EXAMPLES

- Accomplishment
- Achievement
- Advancement
- Adventure
- Attractiveness
- Autonomy
- Authority
- Career
- Caring
- Challenge
- Cleanliness
- Compassion
- Courage
- Creativity
- Determination
- Environment
- Empowerment
- Excitement

- Fame
- Family
- Flexible Schedule
- Focus
- Friendship
- Fun
- Giving
- Goal achievement
- Growth
- Happiness
- Hard work
- Health
- Honesty
- Honor
- Humility
- Integrity
- Intelligence
- Material possessions

- Leadership
- Leisure time
- Love
- Money
- Peace of mind
- Physical fitness
- Popularity
- Power
- Respect
- Responsibility
- Rewarding Work
- Security
- Service
- Socializing
- Spiritual
- Spouse
- Success
- Work Variety

List your values. Prioritize the list.

Organization

Family

Balance

Peace of Mind

Happiness

Health / Physical fitness

Leisure time

Creativity

Env't

Money

Rewarding Work

## Natural Gifts

Who are you? Describe yourself. Make a list of your personal and professional attributes. (Complete this sentence: I am . . .)

_____

_____

_____

_____

_____

_____

_____

_____

_____

_____

_____

_____

_____

_____

_____

_____

_____

_____

Find someone you trust and ask them to list your positive qualities.

What makes you happy?

_Exercise_ _Nature_

_Being outdoors w family_

_Reading_

_art/writing_

_Teaching pts_

Which activities give you the greatest feeling of purpose?

_raising daughters_

_work_

_writing_

_creating anything_

List your strengths. What are your natural talents? What seems to come naturally to you?

What qualities have people complimented you on?

_____

_____

_____

_____

What have people asked you for help doing?

_____

_____

_____

_____

_____

_____

What special knowledge or skills do you possess? This should include
any training or degrees you have achieved. List your skills below:

_____

_____

_____

_____

_____

## *Interest*

What are your interests?

_Cooking_

_Reading / Writing_

_Exercising_

_Art creating_

_____

_____

What do you enjoy doing with your free time when you are not being paid?

_____

_____

_____

_____

_____

What types of books or magazines do you read?

_____

_____

_____

_____

_____

_____

What type of audiotapes or compact disks do you listen to?

_____

_____

_____

_____

Which internet sites do you visit?

_____

_____

_____

_____

What do you collect?

_____

_____

_____

_____

## Relationships

The people you admire are likely to have the same qualities and values you have. List the people you admire and what it is that you admire about them. Do the people you admire have anything in common?

_____

_____

_____

_____

_____

_____

_____

_____

_____

_____

Who is the happiest person you know? Why?

_____

_____

_____

Who is the unhappiest person you know? Why?

_____

_____

_____

Who is the greatest person living? Why?

_____

_____

_____

_____

Who is the worst person living? Why?

_____

_____

_____

_____

Who is the greatest person that has ever lived? Why?

_____

_____

_____

_____

Who is the worst person that has ever lived? Why?

_____

_____

_____

Who are the most valuable people (relationships) in your life?

_____

_____

_____

_____

List the people who admire and respect you. Who are you mentoring?

_____

_____

_____

_____

_____

List the people in your life who recognize your potential.

_____

_____

_____

_____

_____

List the people in your life who love you unconditionally. These are the people who would love you regardless of what you did.

_____

_____

_____

_____

_____

## *Childhood Memories*

What is your most cherished childhood memory?

_vacations - camping trips_

_pasta night_

_movie night_

Which childhood decisions influence your life today?

What did you love doing when you were a child? What were you good at?

_art_

_physical activity /running_

_dancing_

_school_

What did you want to grow up to be?

| | |
|---|---|
| Astronaut | Fashion Designer |
| Space Explorer | Doctor |
| Actress | Detective |

What did you enjoy about school?

Art

Learning new things - any topic

Dancing

Track + Field

What were your hobbies?

Arts

Sewing

Reading / Writing

## *Accomplishments*

List your achievements. Rank these in order of importance. What have you done that you are proud of?

_____

_____

_____

_____

_____

_____

_____

_____

_____

_____

_____

_____

_____

_____

_____

_____

_____

_____

_____

_____

_____

_____

_____

_____

_____

_____

_____

_____

_____

_____

_____

_____

_____

_____

_____

_____

_____

_____

What is your greatest accomplishment?

_____

_____


What skills or strengths did you use in the accomplishment? What part of the accomplishment was most enjoyable? This can give you clues as to what will give your life enjoyment and meaning. Guide your life toward those experiences.

_____

_____

_____

_____


What do you dislike doing? Why?

_____

_____

_____

_____


List what has hurt you.

_____

_____

_____

_____

List the greatest failures in your life. What did you learn from each incident?

_poor mngt of injuries_

What are your fears?

_Fear of Obesity_
_aging_

What are your limiting beliefs?

_Old is not sexy_

What have you wanted to do, but were afraid to try? Is there a dream you have always wanted? Has someone or something kept you from pursuing the dream? What was the dream?

What is the most dangerous risk you have taken? Did you learn anything from taking the risk?

_____

_____

_____

_____

Are there any risks that you are avoiding? If so, what are they?

_____

_____

_____

_____

_____

_____

List all the things that bother you and cause you to worry. List the solution that will bring you peace of mind.

_____

_____

_____

_____

_____

_____

What is not working in your life? List the challenges in your life.

_Paper work_

_Over subscribing myself_

_Financial Security_

_____

_____

_____

List everything that is unfinished in your life. These are the things that clutter your life and drain your energy. These include unfinished business, relationships, and material items that have out lived their usefulness.

_De Clutter Sewing room_

_Photo consolidation_

_"Contacts" Cleansing_

_____

_____

_____

_____

_____

_____

_____

_____

List all the positive and negative events in your life in chronological order on a continuum. List the magic moments, the happy memories and the life experience that have changed and impacted your life. What did you learn from each experience?

_____

_____

_____

_____

_____

_____

_____

_____

_____

_____

_____

_____

_____

_____

_____

_____

_____

## *Summary*

- Increase your self-awareness by answering the questions and exercises in this chapter.
- Use the answers to define your wants and contemplate your life's purpose.
- The self-discovery process defines who you are, your foundation. When you know your foundation, you can move ahead with action.

# DEFINING YOUR WANTS

## Brainstorming Balanced Goals

A balanced life is essential for health and happiness. Short and long term goals should be developed for all areas of your life. This will keep you balanced. Set aside a few hours, go to a quiet place, and start thinking about what you want. During this brainstorming session, don't put limitations on yourself.

> *The true worth of a man is to be measured by the objects he pursues.*
> MARCUS AURELIUS (ROMAN EMPEROR 80-121)

## Analyze Your Life

Assess your life. Using a continuum from one through ten—with one as needing improvement and ten as being fulfilled and satisfied—estimate your success in the following categories. A low number could indicate a category of your life is out of balance and may need development.

### CATEGORIES OF LIFE

Date: _____

- Career          _8_
- Happiness   _7_
- Social          _6_
- Family          _7_

- Health        _7_
- Spiritual     _7_
- Financial    _3_
- Mental        _5_

## *List Your Wants*

What would you do with your life if you knew you could not fail?
If you had no limitations, what would you do with your life? How
would you change? How would you live? What would you be?
What would you have? Create a detailed mental image of the things
you would do and buy. Dream big, make sure these long-term
goals are exciting, and make them take 10 or 20 years to reach.

List what you want to do.

*Finish my book*

List everything you want to be.

_____

_____

_____

_____

_____

_____

_____

_____

_____

_____

_____

_____

_____

_____

_____

_____

_____

_____

_____

List all the places you would like to visit.

_____

_____

_____

_____

_____

_____

_____

_____

_____

_____

_____

_____

_____

_____

_____

_____

_____

_____

List what you want to learn.

_____

_____

_____

_____

_____

_____

_____

_____

_____

_____

_____

_____

_____

_____

_____

_____

List everything you want to have.

_____

_____

_____

_____

_____

_____

_____

_____

_____

_____

_____

_____

_____

_____

_____

_____

_____

_____

_____

## *Sort Your Wants*

Sort the above lists of items into the following areas of your life:

- Career
- Happiness
- Social
- Family

- Health
- Spiritual
- Financial
- Mental

**Career Goals**

_____

_____

_____

_____

_____

_____

_____

_____

_____

_____

_____

_____

_____

_____

## Happiness Goals

_____

_____

_____

_____

_____

_____

_____

_____

_____

_____

_____

_____

_____

_____

_____

_____

_____

_____

_____

_____

## Social Goals

_____

_____

_____

_____

_____

_____

_____

_____

_____

_____

_____

_____

_____

_____

_____

_____

_____

_____

_____

## Family Goals

_____

_____

_____

_____

_____

_____

_____

_____

_____

_____

_____

_____

_____

_____

_____

_____

_____

## Health Goals

_____

_____

_____

_____

_____

_____

_____

_____

_____

_____

_____

_____

_____

_____

_____

_____

_____

_____

## Spiritual Goals

_____

_____

_____

_____

_____

_____

_____

_____

_____

_____

_____

_____

_____

_____

_____

_____

_____

_____

_____

# Financial Goals

_____

_____

_____

_____

_____

_____

_____

_____

_____

_____

_____

_____

_____

_____

_____

_____

_____

_____

_____

## Mental Goals

_____

_____

_____

_____

_____

_____

_____

_____

_____

_____

_____

_____

_____

_____

_____

_____

_____

_____

_____

_____

_____

## *Refining The List*

### Step 1
Review the sorted list and compare it with the areas of your life that need improvement. Where are you out of balance? What is missing from your life? Do the areas that need improvement have only a few goals listed? If so, rethink the issue and develop additional goals.

### Step 2
Review the list of wants; look for items which are incompatible. Compare them and resolve any discrepancies. You cannot go in two different directions at the same time.

### Step 3
Remove from the list things that you are only casually interested in. Keep only the items you really want and are willing to work for. Remember, you can always put the items back on the list, if you really want them.

### Step 4
Estimate the time it will take you to complete each item and write it next to the goal. Now prioritize the goal list. Select the one goal that is the most important for you for each time frame. It might turn out the one goal would accomplish many of the items on your goal list.

## *Summary*
- Brainstorm all the things you want to, do, be, visit, learn, or have.
- Create a list of what you want in your life. Pay particular attention to areas of your life that are not balanced.
- Examine your life for balance. Sort and refine the list to determine the items you really want.
- The items you have identified will be used to program your subconscious mind.

# THE POWER OF PURPOSE

### The Benefits Of Having A Life's Purpose

People who succeed in life have a purpose. They feel good about themselves, are self-confident, and are in control of their lives. They know what they want and have developed a plan to get it. They enjoy the journey. Research has revealed that people with a purpose live happier, more satisfied lives.

Without a purpose, you will defuse your energy, achieve less, and have a tendency to take paths that send you in different directions. If there are no goals, the energy within the mind is wasted. Many people go through life aimlessly and accomplish little. They drift without a destination and end up lost.

You will give your life direction and purpose when you determine what you want and where you are going. Keep your goal foremost in your mind. Select a single life's purpose and focus all of your energy and effort on achieving it. When your life's purpose is known, you will be on the right path and have the drive and energy to obtain it. Make discovering your life's purpose your highest priority!

> *Many persons have a wrong idea of what constitutes true happiness.*
> *It is not attained through self-gratification but through fidelity to*
> *a worthy purpose.*
>       HELEN KELLER (AMERICAN BLIND/DEAF AUTHOR 1880-1968)

## Determining Your Life's Purpose

You have interest and talents that no one else has. Everyone on the earth is different. Work through the exercises in this book and use them to identify your gifts, talents, and interests. Your life's purpose is something that you are naturally gifted at as well as something you love.

It is often very difficult to discover your life's purpose. If you are in a state of confusion, allow time to think through what it is you really want. It can take a few weeks or even months for the answer to surface in your mind. Grow gradually and naturally towards what you want. Take little steps at first, start moving in the right direction. You are likely to receive encouragement and will be making progress towards your goal. If you experience some setbacks, learn from them and continue on your path. Your character will benefit from the attempts. Your destiny is determined by the decisions you make daily. Your life up to this point has prepared you for the path you will take in the future. Learn from the past and direct your life to those things you enjoy doing.

In order to get what you want, it is necessary to clearly define what it is that you want. This is harder than it sounds. Look around you: you will see people that have answered this question differently. Some have chosen to obtain a tangible possession or a position of power. Others have dedicated their lives to their families, or helping others. Still others have chosen to love God and prepare for salvation.

> *Every person above the ordinary has a certain mission that they*
> *are called to fulfill.*
>       JOHANN WOLFGANG VON GOETHE (GERMAN POET 1749-1832)

# LIFE'S MEANING

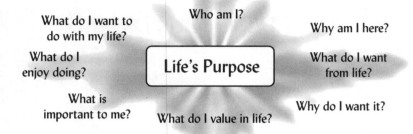

What do I want to do with my life?

Who am I?

Why am I here?

What do I enjoy doing?

**Life's Purpose**

What do I want from life?

What is important to me?

What do I value in life?

Why do I want it?

You are the only person who can answer these questions. When you discover the answers, your life will have direction and meaning and erupt with change. Everyone asks themselves these questions at some point in their lives. Do it sooner, rather than later. This is when life becomes fulfilling and enjoyable.

## The Answers Are Within

You are part of an orderly universe that has a purpose for your life. Often, it is necessary to seek your purpose by meditating and following intuitive guidance. Discovering your life's purpose is a spiritual experience that is inspired by God. As such, it is concerned with love, giving, and serving, not what you receive back. If you search for your life's purpose, you will find it. It is within you already. Find it, and you will be on the path to happiness. When your life's purpose is known, do whatever is needed to protect it, and take steps to bring it into reality. To keep the dream alive, work with it as often as possible. It will become your goal and mission in life. *Share the joy of living*

# IDENTIFYING YOUR DREAMS

What is keeping you from making your dream reality?

What do you have to do to make your dream reality?

What would you do with your life if you knew you would not fail?

What do you really want?

What do you fear, to make this come true?

If you do it, what kind of person will you become?

What will your life be like if you keep doing what you are doing?

What will you become?

> *If you deliberately plan to be less than you are capable of being, then I warn you that you will be unhappy for the rest of your life. You'll be evading your own capabilities, your own possibilities.*
> ABRAHAM MASLOW (AMERICAN PSYCHOLOGIST 1908-1970)

## Mortality

Your time on earth has limits. To get the most out of life, you need to ponder the question, "What do I want to do with the rest of my life?"

What do you want to accomplish before you die?

Finish Book

Travel internationally

Volunteer - mercy ships?

- Raise well-balanced daughters

- Keep nourishing a healthy marriage

- Finish large paintings

What will you have to do to bring this to reality?

- work fewer hours/week

- do more paper work at work

- more disposable income

Write your eulogy. What would you like the people who know you to say when your life comes to an end? What accomplishments do you want to be remembered for?

_____

_____

_____

_____

_____

_____

_____

_____

_____

_____

## Personal Mission Statement

Once your life's purpose is known, write a mission statement. It can be something as noble as being the best parent or spouse possible. This statement will change as you grow and progress through life. It needs to be foremost in your mind and reviewed often. Having a clearly defined purpose or mission allows you to stay focused. When you are faced with major life decisions you can ask, "Will this keep me on purpose?" Always stay on purpose!

Don't be reluctant to declare a mission statement. If the mission statement doesn't fit, it can always be changed. It should be flexible.

For each facet of your life, develop goals to support the mission. For each goal, develop steps to accomplish it. When you work at these activities, you are making progress towards accomplishing your mission or life's purpose.

The fact that you want these things means you can have them. God does not allow you to want with burning desire, without giving you the means to achieve. The power within will respond and give it to you. Natural talent is not needed when you are on a mission. You will be doing God's work. You will successfully pass through any obstacle encountered. Allow growth and abundance into your life. Adopt the attitude that God is your co-creator. Allow him to plan and guide your life. Trust God and follow your intuition.

> *Singleness of purpose is one of the chief essentials for success in life, no matter what may be one's aim.*
> JOHN D. ROCKEFELLER (AMERICAN INDUSTRIALIST 1839-1937)

What is your mission statement? Write it out now!
My mission in life is . . .

_____

_____

_____

You will know when you have found your life's purpose. It will be difficult to achieve, but realizing that it is possible will excite you. You will feel its presence in your body; it is heart felt, as you rise to the challenges. It will just feel right!

## *Summary*

- Determine your life's purpose. You must know what you want in order to get it.
- When you can clearly define your life's purpose, you can achieve it.
- Keep thinking about the question, "What do you want in your life?" Consult your intuition. It will guide you in the right direction. The answers are within.

# THE PERFECT CAREER

The secret to career selection is for you to be interested and challenged by the work you do. When you are working at something you enjoy, the work is easier, and the results are better. Do not settle for employment that is not fulfilling. It doesn't matter what you do, as long as you enjoy it. If you like your job, there is a high probability you will be good at it and this will bring fulfillment.

## CAREER SELECTION CRITERIA

✔ Use your natural talent.

✔ A love for the work.

✔ A sense of mission to provide meaning and fulfillment.

✔ Do what you know; use the skills you already have

*Choose a job you love, and you will never work a day in your life.*
CONFUCIUS (CHINESE PHILOSOPHER 551-479 BC)

## *Employment*

If you are dissatisfied with your work, there is a good chance your job's working conditions are not aligned with your values. You are the only one who can judge the situation.

What is important to you in a career? What are your work values? Prioritize the list.

_____

_____

_____

_____

_____

Do you enjoy the work environment at your place of employment?

Yes _____                    No _____

Are you making enough money?

Yes _____                    No _____

What is it about your work that you like?

_____

_____

_____

_____

What is it about your work that you dislike?

_____

_____

_____

For each job you have held, answer the following questions: What did you enjoy most about the job? What skills did you learn and use in the job?

_____

_____

_____

_____

_____

_____

_____

_____

_____

_____

What would you have to do, to change your present job to increase job satisfaction?

_____

_____

_____

_____

_____

_____

Prioritize a list of the things you enjoy doing.

_____

_____

_____

_____

_____

List the ways you could make a living doing these things.

_____

_____

_____

_____

_____

What work do you consider meaningful?

_____

_____

_____

_____

_____

What work conditions and qualities would be present in your perfect job?

_____

_____

_____

_____

List the people who have suggested career paths for you. Write down their suggestions.

_____

_____

_____

_____

_____

Brainstorm. Make a list of all the careers that appeal to you. What is it about each job that appeals to you?

_____

_____

_____

_____

_____

_____

## Dislikes/Improvements

Often, you can determine what you like by identifying what you don't like. Analyze the careers you dislike and change the negative qualities into positive ones. For instance, if you determine you don't like working outdoors in inclement weather, write the opposite, which is working indoors. Many of the qualities may already be listed above. If you discovered more, add them to the list of qualities that would be present in your perfect work.

List all the careers that do not appeal to you. Determine the qualities you really dislike. List the opposite positive qualities.

_____

_____

_____

_____

_____

_____

_____

_____

## Career Selection

It is easier to select a career when you acknowledge and understand your aptitude, natural talent, values, and desires. Get in touch with your interests and look for employment opportunities. Continually ask yourself, what it is you want? Start working immediately to clarify your goals. If you think long and hard enough, you will know what you should be doing.

> *All things will be produced in superior quantity and quality, and with greater ease, when each man works at a single occupation, in accordance with his natural gifts . . .*
>                          PLATO (GREEK PHILOSOPHER 427-347 BC?)

## Modeling

Study role models; identify people who have achieved what you want. Use them as a model to guide and encourage you to complete your goal. Model them and repeat their success. Try to take on the self-image of the person. Imagine, through their eyes, what it would be like doing what they do. Picture handling the challenges, as well as the glory, associated with the work. What kind of person will you have to be in order to complete your goal? Identify the beliefs, attitudes, personal characteristics, and skills you will have to develop.

Any career you are considering needs to be investigated. Try to find someone doing what you want to do and interview him or her. Be prepared for the interview. Ask questions that will help you discover what the individual did to become successful. Find out all the positive and negative aspects of the job. You will find that most people will share stories of their success with people who are genuinely interested. Make him or her your mentor. Use this information to help you plan the route needed for a similar achievement.

## Making Career Decisions

Career decisions can be one of the most difficult, challenging, and important choices you will encounter in life. This section will give you guidance to make a well thought out decision.

### Step 1

When you are faced with difficult decisions, ask yourself:
"What do I really want?"
"What will make me happy?"
"Is this aligned with my values?"

**Step 2**

List your options/alternatives. Be sure to consider taking no action as an alternative.

**Step 3**

Evaluate the alternatives.

**Step 4**

Go to a quiet place, take one of the career choices and imagine what it would be like in that setting. Try to feel what it would be like in the job. Sense the emotions.

**Step 5**

Think through the following questions: How will you learn the job? Look at the career long term, such as what it will be like in 10 or 20 years. Will the work challenge you long term? Talk with the mature workers in the field and get their insights. Are they happy?

> *The highest reward for a person's toil is not what he gets for it, but what he becomes by it.*
> JOHN RUSKIN (BRITISH CRITIC 1819-1900)

## Choosing Between Two Careers

If you are choosing between two jobs or careers, use a large poster board as a focal point, to keep relevant information pertaining to the decision. Keep the following information on it:

- List each job with its advantages and disadvantages.
- List any information that is related to the decision.
- Identify questions you need answered to clarify any issues about which you are not clear.
- List your mission statement and long term goals.
- List your values. When you are choosing a career, it is important to be aware of your values. If you clearly understand your prioritized values, you will know which job to choose.
- List any comments about the alternatives.

- Highlight your major concerns about your career choices and list any thoughts you have on those issues.
- Review all of the above information. It will provide you with insight to make the decision.

> *When you cannot make up your mind which of two evenly balanced courses of action you should take - choose the bolder.*
> W. J. SLIM (BRITISH FIELD MARSHAL 1891-1970)

## Solving Difficult Problems

One way to solve complex problems is to turn them over to your subconscious mind. Just before going to sleep, define the problem and ask your subconscious for the answer. Often, you will have the solution the very next morning. Give your mind all the known facts and information regarding the challenge. Let the subconscious mind mull over the information, and it will respond with the right answer. It may take several nights for the subconscious mind to provide the answer. It should come before the pending deadline. Have faith and believe in this power. When Thomas Edison had a problem, he would sleep.

> *Problems unsolved when we go to bed are found solved in the morning when we wake.*
> WILLIAM JAMES (AMERICAN PSYCHOLOGIST/PROFESSOR 1842-1910)

When you decide on a career, answer the following questions:
- Does this further my life's purpose?
- Is it aligned with my values?
- Does it utilize my interests and abilities?
- Look at the people doing the work. Is this the type of person you want to become?
- Are the compensation and benefits acceptable?
- Will I enjoy the work environment?

If you can truthfully answer positively to all of the above questions, go for it! Start working towards the change. Take the shortest, most direct route possible to obtain it. Investigate the career and determine exactly what is required to enter it. Do not pursue a degree unless it is absolutely needed.

> *First say to yourself what you would be, and then do what you have to do.*
>                               EPICTETUS (PHILOSOPHER 50-120)

Know the risk, and evaluate the cost. If you make up your mind to go for it, do it, and ignore all the negative comments of well-meaning friends and family. You only live once and you should be the one who determines what that will be.

## Take Action

Take responsibility; don't be afraid to make a decision. To be reluctant to make a decision is to invite failure. If you fail or avoid making a decision, you are actually making a decision that will affect your future. If you make a mistake, learn from it and move on. Life is for living, and living involves some risk, and ultimately, some mistakes.

It will probably be necessary to give up something in order to get what you want. Sometimes, this means you must move out and on. You will likely have to switch employers and/or move to obtain career fulfillment. Only you know what is working in your life.

Many people spend time finding the right career and then fail to follow through and make the switch. If you feel comfortable with the decision, you would be wise to switch. Ultimately, you must make a decision. Take calculated risks and face your fears. This requires resolve and courage. It is also when life becomes fun and enjoyable.

## Career Search

If you are still having difficulty determining your perfect work, here are some helpful ideas to help you with your career search:

- Take personality profiles, interest questionnaires, or aptitude tests to further define your interest.
- Review career search materials at the local library.
- Solicit career ideas from family and friends.
- Take a career exploration course at a local college or university.
- Consult with professional counselors who can assist you with your job search.

## Summary

- Strive for work you love and enjoy doing.
- Identify your natural gifts and talents.
- Align the values identified in the Self Discovery chapter with the career.
- Meditate for guidance on how to use those skills in a career.
- When you are faced with difficult life decisions, turn the problem over to the subconscious mind. The answers are within.
- When you determine which career you would like, extensively research and investigate that field's barriers to entry.
- Model people that who have achieved the success you want. Do what they have done to achieve similar success.
- Take action!

# GOALS -
# PLANNING YOUR LIFE

The mind has a built-in goal-seeking mechanism, which will give you answers and search for solutions to your problems. It acts like a magnet that attracts the events and circumstances needed to accomplish your goal. Your mind must have a clear goal or target of what you want.

When you focus your mind on a clear goal, have faith that your Creative Power will cause it to occur. Start planning and taking steps to reach your objective. Think about your goal constantly and do everything you can to start the process of its achievement. If the goal you are trying to achieve is large, it will change and evolve as it takes shape. Let go of all doubt, fear, and self-centered anxiety. "Believe" you will achieve the goal.

Goals focus your mental energy on a specific path. Concentrating and focusing your mind on a single purpose will intensify your desire and lead you to achieve the goal. Well thought-out goals will drive you into the future. Spend time deliberately designing your future. Take control of your life by setting large, challenging goals.

*You will become as small as your controlling desire; as great as your dominant aspiration.*
JAMES ALLEN (BRITISH BORN AMERICAN AUTHOR 1864-1912)

## *Planning - Start With The End In Mind*

Planning is absolutely essential for you to achieve what you want from life. Develop a plan to bring your goal into reality. Put the plan on paper and review and revise it often. Use the same detail an architect would use to design a home. Think through what you would need to do, be, or have in order to achieve it. Start with the end in mind and incrementally back up, step by step, until you get to today. Create a list of sub-goals. Set deadlines; estimate the amount of time it will take to accomplish the major milestones along the way. Large, long-term goals require planning, hard work, and resources to bring them to fruition.

Use a large poster board to list all the steps needed to achieve your goal. It will act as a focal point for the plan. Cross off each step, when it is completed. When you are not sure what to do, go to the board and determine your next step. If an item on the board is too large, break it down into smaller steps. This will give you steps which you can work on all the time. Be sure the plan has steps that can be taken immediately. Focus on achieving one small piece of the plan, until it is accomplished. Start working on the project and on achieving the smaller items. Bit by bit, bring your large goal into reality.

Be sure your plan is flexible and allows for change. Review and update your plan regularly. Many of the steps you originally recorded may not be needed or there may be easier ways to accomplish them. Your wants will likely change with time. You are not locked into a goal: if it no longer fits, revise or discard it. Make sure you are focusing on what you want.

Work on your goal everyday. Knowing that you are making progress toward your goal will increase your confidence. Look forward to the future with anticipation. Without goals, life can become monotonous. Let the future pull you in the planned direction of your goal.

> *A journey of a thousand miles must begin with a single step.*
> LAO TZU (CHINESE PHILOSOPHER 604-531 B.C.)

## Value Of Goals

In 1953, Yale University conducted a study that proves the value of goals. They asked their seniors if they had clear, specific, written goals, as well as plans to achieve them. Three percent of the students said they did. Twenty years later, they re-interviewed the surviving members of the class. They discovered that the people with goals had a combined net worth that surpassed the rest of the students. The evaluators concluded that the goal setters were happier, more satisfied with life, and had better personal relationships.

## Personal Goal Setting Guidelines

- The goals you set should challenge you and make you stretch. These goals should require you to expand your abilities and force you to grow. Most people set their goals too low. It is better to set your goals high and miss, than to set them too low and achieve little.

- Goals need to be worth all the effort and work they require. Research how much work is involved in achieving what you want. Identify the knowledge, support, and training you will need to accomplish the goal.

- Understand why you want the goal, and know the benefits of achieving it. Strong reasons for wanting the goal will create the drive and energy to see it through. Look forward with enthusiasm. This will help you to overcome obstacles, and complete the goal. When you really want something, you will find a way to bring it into reality. Great reasons accomplish great things!

- Have faith and believe you can accomplish your goal. Inwardly know that you are capable of achieving it. Working for something while believing you are not capable of achieving it won't work. Know exactly what you want and believe you can obtain it, otherwise you will be sending out mixed signals and cause confusion. Your goal must be affirmed with conviction. If you doubt your abilities, your subconscious mind will know that, and the result will be failure. The goal-seeking mechanism is self-regulated. People do not commit to goals they are not capable of achieving.

- Take action! Start immediately to attain your goal. Work on first things first; always keep in mind where you want to go. Commit to achieving your goal and do whatever it takes to accomplish it.

- Goals need to be in harmony with other goals. Goals that are aligned with each other will be achieved easier and faster. Goals need to maintain your integrity, agree with any deep-seated beliefs, and not conflict with your values. Your goals should not cause you emotional conflict. Set goals so they are consistent with your life's purpose. Goals that are aligned with your life's purpose are very powerful!

- Make your goal measurable. Examine where you are and what is needed to achieve your goal. Remember, what gets measured gets done!

- Set deadlines, reward yourself and celebrate when you accomplish major parts of the goal on time. Rewards help you to stay motivated.

- Keep your goals private. Do not disclose your goals to people who are likely to belittle or impede you. Tell your immediate family and only those whom you think will encourage and help you. You will need their support.

- Prior to achieving your goal, start planning another goal. When you accomplish your goal, you will lose enthusiasm, burning desire, and will level off. You will find that you are at your best when you are achieving challenging goals. Don't allow much rest between accomplishments. Savor the achievement, but don't flatten out.

## Summary

- Develop large, exciting, ambitious goals. Make them your future destination.
- Start with the end in mind and develop a plan to achieve it.
- Commit to your goal; resolve to do whatever it takes.
- Believe you can accomplish it.
- Develop a burning desire for your goal and it will materialize.

# UNIVERSAL LAWS OF LIFE

The universe operates in harmony with, and is governed by, laws. These laws are comparable to scientific standards. They are unyielding, inviolable, and will work for anyone. They can work for you or against you. Your understanding of these laws determines your success. When you know and apply them, your life will change. They are the keys to happiness and abundance in life.

Often you will see people who are basically good having many challenges in their life. A closer examination will reveal that they do not understand these laws. Misunderstanding them will bring disaster. If you are impoverished, demand more from life. Abundance is there for the taking. It is up to you to accept it; put these principles to work.

## Law Of Cause And Effect

There is a reason for everything that happens in your life. Every occurrence, event, or state is contingent upon a prior occurrence, event, or state. You can bring into your life what you desire by identifying and repeating the cause. Conversely, if things are occurring in your life that you want eliminated, you can identify the cause and work to remove it. There are many people who are not happy with their lives and, for whatever reason, choose to live the same way. If you keep doing the same things day after day, you will get the same results. Understand and recognize this law so you can create the cause, which delivers the effect you desire.

> *Shallow people believe in luck and circumstances; Strong people believe in cause and effect.*
> RALPH WALDO EMERSON (AMERICAN POET/ESSAYIST 1803-1882)

## Law Of Attraction

This is a simple law. You will attract into your life what you give out. Like always attracts like: a smile brings a smile, love brings you love, kindness brings you kindness, etc. Always affirm good thoughts. Positive thoughts attract positive experiences into your life. The subconscious mind creates these things for you.

This works the same with positive as with negative thoughts. Give out love, beauty, truth, and friendship and it will come back to you. Give out evil and hatred, and it will return. If you harm, hurt or cheat another, this will come back to you someday.

> *There is a universal law in the mental realm, "like always attracts like"*
> CLAUDE BRISTOL (AMERICAN AUTHOR 1891-1951)

## The Power Of Thought

Your present thoughts determine your future. You are living in a world of cause and effect. Thought is the cause and everything else is the effect. Few things happen by accident. Your thoughts have caused most of what has happened to you. Thought always precedes action, creating the concept or object. To get what you want, program thoughts and pictures of the desired result into your mind.

> *You become what you think about.*
> EARL NIGHTINGALE (AMERICAN AUTHOR/SPEAKER 1921-1989)

## Thoughts Create

Everything that has ever been created was first a thought. Activate the creative process of the mind by visualizing a goal with belief and faith of its accomplishment, and the mind will work relentlessly to achieve it. If thoughts are repeated frequently, they will eventually be believed as true. What your conscious mind acknowledges as truth, your subconscious mind will bring into reality. Whatever you can imagine can be created in your life.

This force can work for you or against you. It brings both good and bad thoughts into your life. Moral and virtuous thoughts will produce positive results. Evil and sinister thoughts will produce negative results. If your thoughts have been consumed by failure, fear, and doubt, those thoughts will be brought to you. Never think about fear or what you don't want to happen. Negative thoughts of failure will bring you failure.

A person who thinks of sickness is always sick. A person who thinks he is accident-prone, is in a lot of accidents. A person who thinks he is always late, is always late. The dominating thoughts that occupy your mind will control who and what you will be. Many people are unaware of this power. They are unknowingly drawing toward them the object of their thoughts. You have control of your thoughts and, because of this, you can mold and shape your character, life, and direct your destiny. Start affirming and visualizing what you desire.

The uncontrolled conscious mind allows random thoughts into the subconscious mind. Thoughts suddenly appear and leave. You have the choice to either accept them or quickly dismiss them. Negative thoughts should be cast out immediately. If you allow stray, negative thoughts in and out of your mind, you can expect undesirable things to come back to you. Control what is going in! Affirm positive thoughts and the negative ones will cease.

Your life on the outside is a reflection of your inner thoughts. Your thoughts and feelings have made you the person you are today.

They determine who you are and build your character. To be happy and positive, think pleasant and optimistic thoughts. Conversely, to be dismal and negative, think depressing and pessimistic thoughts. Whether you are optimistic or pessimistic will depend on your thoughts. If you change your thoughts, you will change your life. Permanent change starts on the inside.

The Creative Power within will bring you what you desire. If you think positive thoughts, positive events will occur. Your wishes will be granted, if you clearly visualize consistently and confidently. Always dwell on thoughts that will benefit and build you. Thoughts of beauty, tranquility, friendship, and love will bring you a joyful life.

> *Whatsoever things are true, whatsoever things are honest, whatsoever things are just, whatsoever things are pure, whatsoever things are lovely, whatsoever things are of good report; if there be any virtue, and if there be any praise, think on these things.*
> PAUL THE APOSTLE (PHILIPPIANS 4:8)

## Cultivate Your Mind

The mind is often compared to a garden: it can be cultivated or neglected. When planted with seeds, fertilized, and tended, it will produce the desired crop. If it is neglected, it will attract and yield weeds. A thought is like a seed: whatever you plant in your mind will be brought forth. Control your thoughts, consistently affirm them, and you will bring forth the desired crop. However, if you allow random thoughts and outside influences to enter your mind, it will yield weeds. If you plant an acorn, you will get an oak tree. If you consistently hold a thought in your mind, your mind will manifest the desired result into your life.

The best way of controlling your mind is through a mission or life's purpose. When you follow a plan to achieve a mission, you will direct your thought in a positive way. If you study the life of any person who is successful, you will find that he or she has consciously or unconsciously used this formula. Achievement is not possible without mind control. First see in your mind what you want to create, then bring it into reality.

> *Thoughts allied fearlessly to purpose becomes creative force. . .*
> JAMES ALLEN (BRITISH BORN AMERICAN AUTHOR 1864–1912)

## Summary

- Laws govern our universe.
- The universe has unlimited abundance. Learn its ways and use its laws.
- Everything occurs for a reason. Identify and bring into your life the cause and effect you want.
- You get back what you give out. Like begets like.
- Thoughts are creative; positive thoughts build, negative thoughts destroy.
- The subconscious mind creates the thoughts that are held in the conscious mind. A thought repeated and consistently held clearly in your mind will become reality.

# SPIRITUAL POWER

An acorn seed contains everything it needs to be a mighty oak. It is self-contained, and does not need outside forces to shape its final destiny. Unseen potential is released through the miracle of life. All it takes to nurture it is time, sun, and water. You are self-contained, like the seed: the creator gave you everything you need to succeed. You are much greater than an acorn seed!

Within you is a spiritual power that you can consult when you are confronted with life's problems. You have access to, and are linked with, universal knowledge. Wise people throughout the ages have believed that our minds are linked to a universal intelligence. Thomas Edison knew that many of his ideas came from an outside source. He is quoted as saying "ideas are in the air."

> *There is one mind common to all individual men.*
> RALPH WALDO EMERSON (AMERICAN POET/ESSAYIST 1803-1882)

Everyone has his or her own understanding of God. Regardless of what religion you practice, you will recognize that there is a Divine Power, a Life Force that exists in all living things. This power is known by many names, including Superconscious Mind, Universal Mind, Creative Intelligence, Higher Power, and Spirit. Most call it God. Your inner voice and intuition are connected to this Divine Power. Know you can consult God, and he will give you guidance.

> *God has many names though He is only one Being.*
> ARISTOTLE (GREEK PHILOSOPHER 384-322 BC)

# The Divine Power

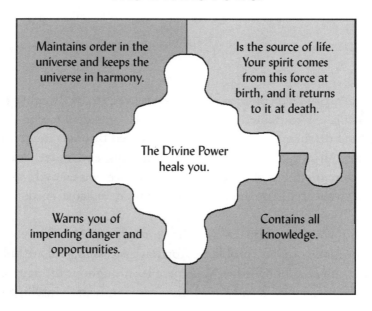

Maintains order in the universe and keeps the universe in harmony.

Is the source of life. Your spirit comes from this force at birth, and it returns to it at death.

The Divine Power heals you.

Warns you of impending danger and opportunities.

Contains all knowledge.

## *We Are Co-creators Of Our Lives*

The human spirit is connected to the Divine Spirit. It came from this spirit and will rejoin it. Your mind is connected to a source of wisdom, love, beauty, truth, and infinite intelligence. You can consult this power, learn its ways, and use its guidance. The power within is bountiful, endless, and eternal.

God is your father and, just like your biological father, he will work with you to obtain whatever you want. Open your heart and your mind to God. Understand that you are one. He will guide you through life's challenges and opportunities. The greatest revelation you can have is when you realize this power is with you, and will not allow you to fail. When you become aware of this, you can accomplish whatever you want.

> *The kingdom of God is within you.*
>                                                                    JESUS

Your spirit is the object of life! Everything is made from spirit energy. Trust this power, and you will have peace of mind. Fear and worry will be eliminated. You will know the power is an essential part of your success. This power is available to everyone; it has given you everything you need to live a happy and successful life.

> *Without the assistance of the Divine Being . . . I cannot succeed.*
> *With that assistance, I cannot fail.*
>                                                    ABRAHAM LINCOLN
>                 (SIXTEENTH PRESIDENT OF THE UNITED STATES 1809–1865)

## Gratitude

Thank the creative forces of the universe for the abundance in your life. It is mystical how this will help to put into motion the power needed to obtain your goal. It is as though the universe acknowledges the gratitude. When you are genuinely thankful to the creator, this activates forces that cause joy and abundance to flow into your life.

## Intuition

Intuition is a natural mental phenomenon. The mind is given direction without a sound, logical process. Intuition is powerful! It is a key component in developing creative ideas. It guides you, knowing your inner truths. It is the Divine Power giving advice.

Tune into this power; let it fill you with harmony, joy, peace, beauty, and love. The power is accessed through thought, when you meditate. You feel its presence. It intuitively knows what is good for you and will guide and keep you heading in the direction of your goals. The Divine Power has the answers to all of life's questions. When you follow the intuitive voice and feelings, you will be making the right decision.

Anyone can develop his or her intuitive skills. Learn to be friends with it and trust it. Pay attention and monitor situations in which you have received intuitive guidance. Learn from those experiences and trust the wisdom. Move in the direction that feels right. If an activity feels right, it is probably worth doing.

Great thinkers, creative artists, writers, and inventors rely heavily on intuition for guidance with their work. Many business executives acknowledge that their success is a result of developing strong intuitive powers. Successful people, in all walks of life, frequently use their intuitive skills to make decisions. These skills guide them with daily events in their lives. When you trust your intuition, you can accomplish your goals faster. You will experience a life of joy, abundance, and fullness. Believe in this power: it will guide you and answer life's most difficult questions.

Animals have a similar power, which is instinct. Animals have guidance without instructions. They instinctively know how to behave. In one study, three homing pigeon eggs and three rock pigeon eggs were incubated. The pigeons were raised in a cage until they were full-grown, then taken miles from home and let free. The homing pigeons flew home, while the rock pigeons flew to the nearest cliff. Both groups had been raised without parents, so their inner instincts were guiding them.

If the Divine Creator gave this gift to birds, is there any reason to doubt your powers? You have a similar power within you; it will guide you along your path.

> *The only real valuable thing is intuition.*
> ALBERT EINSTEIN (GERMAN BORN AMERICAN PHYSICIST 1879-1955)

## The Divine Inner Voice

The Divine Creator tells you the things he wants you to know. This voice lets you know when your life is not working. It tells you when you are not happy, and when your life is out of balance. It signals you through uneasiness and restless thoughts. It may be telling you that work isn't fun anymore, that you are burning out, getting stuck, not growing, not challenged, or you are ready for a change. This guidance will only occur for a short time. If you ignore it, it will be silenced and leave. You must value the guidance and take steps to change your life. Otherwise, you will adjust to the situation and become complacent. With time, the inner voice urging you to change will quiet. You will lose the incentive to change. Learn to recognize and appreciate your inner voice and it will guide you on the right path. Do whatever it takes to achieve inner peace. Learn to distinguish the Divine inner voice and feelings, which originate from God. Wisdom and guidance are available to you. All you need to do is to be able to distinguish intuition from other mental chatter. Listen to and trust this voice.

When you are facing challenging times in your life, it is wise to consult your inner wisdom. Go within and follow your inner voice: it will correctly guide you. Communication with the Creative Intelligence assures your success. Listen to it and follow the direction. If you go against your intuition, you are usually sorry. This guidance is the only thing that can rescue you and change your life. There is nothing else to follow!

> *Let us be silent that we may hear the whispers of the gods.*
> RALPH WALDO EMERSON (AMERICAN POET/ESSAYIST 1803-1882)

This inner voice is also your conscience. It guides you to do the right thing. It knows when you are virtuous or sinful, and communicates this to you. Living a life of honesty and integrity is essential for happiness.

> *Labor to keep alive in you breast that little spark of celestial fire called conscience.*
> GEORGE WASHINGTON
> (FIRST PRESIDENT OF THE UNITED STATES 1732-1799)

## Summary

- Your mind contains the power to create, heal, and receive guidance from a Higher Power.
- When you use this power wisely, you are able to accomplish extraordinary things.
- The Divine Power responds to the belief you have in him. He will give you whatever you want.
- Trust the inner voice and follow the guidance. It will support you and give you the courage to achieve your goals.
- Take time to appreciate and be grateful for all you have.

# THE MAGIC OF BELIEVING

Your thoughts determine your beliefs, and your beliefs cause your reality. If you believe something is possible, you are likely to accomplish it. Conversely, if you doubt it can be done, you will probably fail. You can only have one belief about a subject or idea. If you have mixed feelings or two beliefs, the subconscious mind will accept the most dominant belief. It is possible to succeed when others don't believe in you. However, you will never be successful unless you believe in yourself.

> *Whosoever shall say unto this mountain, be thou taken up and cast into the sea; and shall not doubt in his heart, but shall believe that what he saith cometh to pass; he shall have it. Therefore I say unto you all things whatsoever ye pray and ask for, believe that ye receive them and ask for, believe that ye receive them and ye shall have them.*
>
> JESUS

## Self-image

Your self-image determines who you are and what you will become. It consists of the beliefs held in the subconscious mind. As you live your life, you encounter many experiences, which are recorded in the subconscious mind. The subconscious mind records the good and the bad. The ideas and life experiences you accept as the truth form your self-image.

Your self-image is the way you view yourself. It is the inner knowledge you have of yourself, such as, "I'm a hard worker", "I'm good with computers", "I'm a good athlete", and "I'm good at mathematics". You have a self-image of your style of dress, how heavy you are, how much you eat, how organized you are and how much money you earn. These inner beliefs control your behavior. You act and behave in a manner that is consistent with the way you see yourself. To be happy and enjoy life, you need a strong self-image. Love, trust, and have faith in yourself.

## Self-image Change

Your self-image is formed by beliefs, which are held in your subconscious mind. In order to change your behavior, you must first change these beliefs. If you believe you are heavy and eat too much, your subconscious will manifest the desired result. You can temporarily override the system with will power, but with time, you will return to the natural, old belief. The only way to enact permanent change is to modify the belief from the inside out.

Self-image is the key to understanding and changing human behavior. You will never be more than the limits held in your subconscious mind. Change the belief, and you will change the behavior. Change the attitudes that are holding you back, and replace them with new, empowering beliefs. Some beliefs become obstacles, restraining you and keeping you from growing. Beliefs can be overwritten. Change your beliefs and you will change your self-image. You created your self-image, and you can change it.

*What you think of yourself is much more important than what others think of you.*
        SENECA (SPANISH BORN ROMAN STATESMAN 4 BC-65 AD)

## *Where Your Beliefs Come From*

You were not born with the beliefs you now have. All of your beliefs are learned. Our family, friends, relatives, teachers, and other authority figures are the source of many of these beliefs. When you accept and internalize their suggestions, they become true for you. You act in accordance with the truth, as you believe it.

### Where Your Beliefs Come From

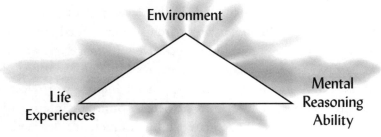

ENVIRONMENT

Life
Experiences

Mental
Reasoning
Ability

*ENVIRONMENT* - When and where you have grown up has created many of your beliefs. Your beliefs would be different if you were raised in the 1930's during the Great Depression, versus if you were raised today. Also, your standard of living was determined by the wealth of your parents. Your beliefs will be different if you were raised in an inner city ghetto, versus an affluent suburb.

*MENTAL REASONING* - Mental abilities are a source of beliefs. We are all given different mental reasoning abilities; some are more capable than others.

*LIFE EXPERIENCES* - If you have been successful in obtaining a difficult goal, you have experienced the skills needed to win. Knowing you have been successful in one venture builds confidence that you can do it again. Successful goal achievement causes one to know deep within that he or she can accomplish and achieve what they want.

If you have tried many things in the past and not experienced success, you will not be able to draw on this valuable resource. It is difficult to overcome self-limiting beliefs. When you believe you can't lose weight, that you lack athletic ability, or whatever else, you are acting out a self-fulfilling prophecy. Your beliefs determine your success!

## Self-image Formation

Your parents played a major role in the development of your self-image. If you had loving, caring parents, they helped you to feel good about yourself, and built a positive self-image. However, if you had parents who had trouble expressing love, were negative and faultfinding, you probably experienced feelings of rejection and depression. These feelings helped to build an inferior self-image. Feeling inept, inadequate, and incompetent is learned!

## Awareness/ False Beliefs

Your present state of awareness is comprised of life experiences and learning. In many areas of your life, you have accepted false beliefs from well meaning friends, relatives, and experts. Your mind has accepted erroneous ideas, which you presently believe to be true. Many of these experiences were distorted when you perceived them. They are not the truth, but your perception of the truth. When the information was recorded in the subconscious mind, it became your truth and it impacted your actions. This is your perception of reality.

When you form this mental picture, it becomes the way you are. You don't question the belief. Most of the time, you cannot even remember the root cause of the belief. Your perception of the situation or event could have been completely in error; however, you perceive the event as if it were true. Often you have trouble seeing everything there is to see. The subconscious mind filters the information to support your dominant belief.

## Self-limiting Ideas

If you see yourself as a "C" student, you will activate the drive and creative energy needed to obtain a "C." If you find yourself getting an "A" on a test, you may automatically correct your way of thinking to get a "C" next time. Your self-image knows you are a "C" student. The opposite is also true. If you get an "F" on a test, you will likely activate the creative energy to bring your grade up. You have to change this image in order for you to consistently get higher grades.

All of us have unknowingly developed and kept beliefs that limit us and hold us back. Examine your life. Are there areas in which you perceive problems? If so, look at your beliefs. They are likely to be the underlying cause. Many of your beliefs lack a foundation of truth. You may have believed an authority figure who made an off-hand comment. If you have accepted the belief that you are awkward, obese, unfit, lazy, or you will always live in poverty, you will likely manifest the desired beliefs.

> *If we did all the things we are capable of, we would literally astound ourselves.*
>
> THOMAS A. EDISON (AMERICAN INVENTOR 1847-1931)

## Comfort Zones

The self-image has set limits that govern your behavior. This maintains your sanity and keeps you acting like you. When you venture out of this comfort zone, doing things that are not normal, you will feel anxiety and stress. It could be parachuting from an airplane, getting a new job, or giving a presentation. If you believe these tasks are not normal behavior and therefore outside of your comfort zone, you will experience anxiety and stress. This is the comfort zone being activated, telling you to get back where you belong.

Personal growth requires you to move beyond your comfort zone. Some people view moving outside of their comfort zone as something to fear. Others know this is part of the growth process and view the experience as an adventure.

## Self-talk

Self-talk is the conversation you have with yourself. You are always talking to yourself, silently in thought. Unfortunately, many of the things you say are very negative and critical. Your beliefs are programmed with self-talk thoughts. The subconscious gives credence to the self-talk and forms a belief. It then directs you to perform as you believe.

Let's look at how beliefs are programmed in your mind. Say, for example, someone calls something you did "stupid." The event will have little meaning, unless you agree with the comment and think, "they're right, what I did was stupid." If the event was embarrassing, you are likely to relive it many times in your mind with emotion. You are programming yourself to accept this new, negative belief. The subconscious will record the original event, and the self-talk replay as though it actually happened.

Now take the same situation and, instead of programming negatively, acknowledge the event and affirm to yourself that you made a mistake and the next time you will do it differently. This is the same situation, but you have internalized it positively to improve future performance.

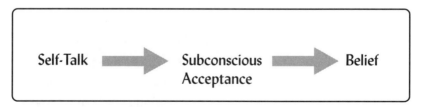

## Positive Self-talk

Anyone can learn to control his or her inner dialogue. It is a learned skill that will change your life. Your future is affected by your self-talk and your thoughts. Eliminate all communication that is negative, demeaning, cynical, nagging, disparaging, and faultfinding. When you start thinking positive, confident, loving thoughts, you will discover that your life will change. Your positive inner world will cause your outer world to change.

Seek your own approval and judge your own abilities. You could wait for others to tell you how good you are, but you will probably discover positive comments are few and far between. Instead, rely on your own self-talk to make positive comments when you do a good job. Be objective when you view your performance, and learn from your mistakes. Learn to accept your own self-praise, and value it over what others say.

## Stand Guard At The Gate

Words are powerful! Say nothing to yourself that you do not want to come true. Control the information that is allowed into your mind. The information that gets through controls your beliefs. Take control of the talk that feeds your mind. When you catch yourself thinking negative self-talk, learn to tell yourself, "Stop it! That's not the way I am, when this occurs again I will . . ." then picture and feel the emotions of perfection.

Stand guard at the gate to your mind and do not let what others say enter and erode your confidence. Be careful of others' comments. People can't hurt your feelings and make you feel bad unless you let them. Deny all negative, destructive talk from others: this will allow you to grow. Choose not to allow anyone to influence you negatively!

*No one can make you feel inferior without your consent.*
ELEANOR ROOSEVELT (AMERICAN FIRST LADY 1884-1962)

Spend a day monitoring your self-talk. When you detect a negative comment, replace it by saying, "That's not like me." Rephrase the criticism, making a positive statement. If you are like most people, you will be amazed by the amount of negative self-talk you regularly give yourself.

## Self Evaluation

The self-image is created; shaped, and nourished by the way you evaluate yourself. It doesn't matter what others say or believe. It only matters what you tell yourself and internalize. If you maintain a positive attitude and really believe and expect the best, you are usually not disappointed. What you expect, you will usually get. This works both ways, positive and negative. Things seem to turn out badly when you expect them to.

Become less and less dependent on external evaluation and more reliant on your own evaluation of your performance. Do not think of others as being more important than you, and don't depend on others for your feeling of worth. Ask yourself whether you are living in a way that pleases you. There is no need to look to others for approval or disapproval.

Whatever you work on, do the job to the best of your abilities. Take responsibility for your actions. If you do something that doesn't turn out the way you want, learn from it. Take responsibility for the decisions you make and don't blame others. Learn from your mistakes and tell yourself, "Next time I will do this differently."

## Expectations

Our expectations of others affect and influence the people around us. The expectations we have for the people who see us as an authority figure will impact their futures. People are likely to live up to expectations we have of them, both good and bad.

Dr. Rosenthal, a Harvard University professor, and Leonore Jacobson, an elementary school principal, conducted a study in 1968. Principal Jacobson told three teachers that they were the best teachers at the school. They were also told they would be teaching the school's gifted children and the principal had high expectations for the coming year. The teachers were instructed that the placement of the children was confidential: the children and parents were not to know.

The teachers were monitored and observed to improve their teaching abilities. At the conclusion of the school year, the teachers were told about the experiment. In reality, they were not given gifted children. The students were randomly chosen from the student population. The teachers were also selected randomly from the staff. The students were tested before and after the experiment, and their academic achievement increased 20 to 30 percent. This outstanding outcome was the result of belief and high expectations.

Parent's expectations for their children have a powerful influence on their lives. If your parents had high expectations for you, it is likely you have tried to achieve for them. This probably resulted in achievement you would have not otherwise had.

## Summary

- Your beliefs shape your behavior. You will achieve what you believe to be true.
- Many of your beliefs were accepted when you were young. After they are established, you rarely question their validity.
- The subconscious mind houses beliefs that make up your awareness level. Self-talk feeds and sustains these beliefs.
- Self-talk influences your self-image. Manage your self-talk, and you can change your life.
- Recognize that Personal growth requires you to move beyond your comfort zone. This will cause anxiety and tension. If you

are going to grow, you have to acknowledge and expand your comfort zone.

- When you can alter your beliefs, you can become whatever you desire.

# THE MIND

There are three aspects of the mind: the conscious, subconscious, and superconscious. The mind is a powerful, reliable resource that is capable of bringing you anything you want. Understand this power and realize its capabilities. It can be directed to draw more out of life.

*All the resources we need are in the mind.*

THEODORE ROOSEVELT
(TWENTY-SIXTH PRESIDENT OF THE UNITED STATES 1858-1919)

## CONSCIOUS MIND

Makes choices                     Source of willpower

Percieves our                     Reviews memory to
present awareness                 determine similar
                                  experiences

The conscious mind perceives, analyzes, reasons, and makes comparisons. It applies the power of choice and is the source of willpower. The information contained in it comes from, and is filtered through, your five senses. The conscious mind recognizes and remembers all bodily, intellectual, and emotional feelings. It reviews memory, to determine similar experiences. The conscious mind screens all data, interprets the truth, and sends it to the subconscious mind.

## SUBCONSCIOUS MIND

Controls bodily functions

Stores all
memory

Handles learned
functions

Holds your
self-image

Goal-seeking
servomechanism

The subconscious mind controls many bodily functions. This includes your heart rate, breathing, digestion, and autonomic nervous system. The subconscious mind never rests. It works while you are awake and when you are sleeping.

The subconscious mind handles learned functions. All new activities are consciously learned first. Through repetition, they gradually switch from conscious activities to subconscious actions.

The subconscious mind stores all of your memories. It records all of the good things you have done, and all the times you acted without virtue. It keeps track of these things, and these acts cause you to feel worthy or worthless, capable or incapable.

The self-image of who you are is held in the subconscious mind. This keeps you behaving in a manner consistent with these beliefs.

The subconscious mind is a goal-seeking servomechanism. It will search, find, and deliver a clearly defined goal. It can be programmed!

The attitudes and beliefs held in the subconscious mind determine who you are and how you live your life. In order to get what you want, your desires must be held in the subconscious mind. The subconscious mind receives suggestions from the conscious mind and goes to work to bring them into your life. The instructions must be clearly defined and visualized with emotion. If they are unclear or mixed, the subconscious mind will not respond. It simply does not know which way to proceed. The subconscious accepts statements literally, without question. It does not rationalize, use common sense, pass judgment, or decline an idea. It will accept failure or success.

The wants of the conscious mind are sometimes frustrated and sabotaged by the negative beliefs in the subconscious mind. They can hold contrasting ideas. When there is disagreement, the subconscious will rule. An example of this is wealth consciousness. If you have a subconscious belief, you are not worthy of wealth, you will never obtain it, even though you may consciously desire wealth. For optimum performance, get the conscious and the subconscious mind working together with the same beliefs.

As soon as you change the inner picture of who you are, you will automatically behave that way. The change will occur without anxiety and stress. When you can clearly see yourself doing and having what you want, your subconscious will do the things needed to bring them into your life.

> *The power to move the world is in your subconscious mind.*
> WILLIAM JAMES (AMERICAN PSYCHOLOGIST/PROFESSOR 1842–1910)

## *Reticular Activating System*

The reticular activating system screens information. You are constantly exposed to lots of stimuli. Information of value is allowed into your mind and recognized. Information viewed as not valuable is screened out. Once you precisely determine what it is you want, this system will automatically allow information of value in. The more specific you are, the better job it will do to screen the appropriate information. Your mind is searching for ways to achieve the goal and bring it into reality.

The best example of this is a crowded social gathering where there is a lot of talking. Someone mentions your name and somehow you hear it. Your awareness suddenly increases and you focus your attention on that conversation. This is your reticular activating system working.

Set goals without knowing all the answers. Trust your reticular activating system. It will turn on your awareness, and the way to accomplish your goal will appear. Most people want to know the answers before they take the risk. If they don't know the answers, they believe, they can't do it. The exact opposite approach is setting the goal without knowing how it will be achieved. Picture the end result, have faith, and know you will accomplish it. Then, let the universe bring it into reality by delivering you the ideas and resources. Achieving your goal will require hard work, but the way will appear. Move toward your goal through action, and enjoy the journey.

# SUPERCONSCIOUS MIND

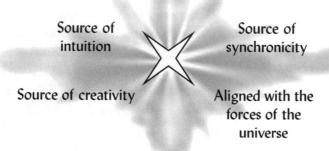

Source of intuition

Source of synchronicity

Source of creativity

Aligned with the forces of the universe

The superconscious mind is the channel/source of your intuition, which is connected to the Higher Power. This power is the source of all knowledge. It is interested in your well-being and will direct you toward your goals. Intuition, wisdom, and guidance are channeled from the Divine Force to direct your life. It is the source of psychic power and synchronicity.

## Synchronicity

Synchronicity is one of the universe's best-kept secrets. This force acts like a magnet to draw into your life the people, situations, and resources to achieve your goal. Program your subconscious mind with success thoughts and the object of the thoughts will manifest in your life. Strange coincidences will start to occur. Seemingly mystical forces, which are present in the universe, will be activated. You will see things you did not see before. People and situations will be brought into your life at the right time in order for you to accomplish your desire.

> *Until one is committed, there is hesitancy, the chance to draw back, always ineffectiveness. Concerning all acts of initiative and creation, there is one elementary truth the ignorance of which kills countless ideas and splendid plans: that the moment one definitely commits oneself, then providence moves too. All sorts of things occur to help one that would never otherwise have occurred. A whole stream of events issues from the decision, raising in one's favor all manner of unforeseen incidents, meetings and material assistance which no man could have dreamed would have come his way. Whatever you can do or dream you can, begin it. Boldness has genius, power and magic in it. Begin it now.*
> JOHANN WOLFGANG VON GOETHE (GERMAN POET 1749-1832)

Look within and receive guidance from the superconscious mind. Know you are connected to the infinite source of power that keeps the world in balance. This power can help you solve all of life's problems. You access it through meditation. Quiet your mind and you will be guided by intuition and feelings. Act on that wisdom, for this is the path you should follow. This power works best when you have faith: believe in this power and experience it often.

## Summary

- The mind is composed of the conscious, subconscious, and the superconscious.
- The conscious mind perceives your present awareness.
- The subconscious mind is programmed by thoughts held in the conscious mind.
- To achieve more out of life, the conscious mind and the subconscious mind need to hold the same belief. If there is disagreement, the subconscious will dominate.
- The superconscious mind links you to Divine guidance. It is interested in your success.
- Synchronicity will bring to you the circumstances and events needed to make your goal reality.

# PROGRAMMING THE MIND

The subconscious mind can be programmed to attract wealth, love, success, and happiness. This is done through a process called "imprinting." Imprinting is the subconscious programming of a goal, using affirmations, brilliant visualization, and charged emotion. Each time you affirm and visualize a goal with emotion, you are experiencing the event as though it occurred. You are using repetition to imprint a goal into the subconscious mind. Once the new goal overwrites the old belief, it will be accepted by the subconscious, and your performance will change. Imprinted goals, affirmed with conviction, create the inner desire to attain the goal.

The human nervous system cannot determine a real experience from a vividly imagined one. Affirmations repeated over and over, combined with emotion, record the concept in the subconscious mind.

*Whatever you vividly imagine, ardently desire, sincerely believe, and enthusiastically act upon, will inevitably happen.*
MAXWELL MALTZ (AMERICAN AUTHOR 1899-1975)

## Affirmations

An affirmation is a statement of belief, affirming it is so. Affirmations are thoughts, and when they are repeated frequently, they become beliefs. With repetition, the mind will accept a statement as truth. Affirmations can be said aloud or said silently in thought. Affirmations are an easy and simple way to program the mind.

> *Those who really seek the path to enlightenment dictate terms to their mind. Then they proceed with strong determination.*
> BUDDHA (568-488 BC)

## Affirmation Guidelines

- Affirmations should be stated in the first person and in the present tense. Always word affirmations as though they are true. This is usually done using the words "I am". Never use the terms, "I will," "I could," "I can," or "I am able to." These phrases imply doubt.

- Affirmations need to be positively worded and should state the attribute you want. They should not mention the habit or characteristic you want to get rid of. For example, if you say, "I am not fearful," you are likely to picture yourself being fearful. Instead, the affirmation should be stated, "I am courageous". By doing this, you send your mind a positive picture.

- Affirmations should be brief. Try to make your affirmations simple, easy to remember, and action-oriented. Use words you are comfortable with.

- Affirmations need to be specific and worded as though they have been achieved. Know exactly what you want. Do not make general statements, such as, "I am wealthy". Instead,

define a specific net worth. Affirmations should focus on the
end result.

- Affirmations said with enthusiasm, emotion, and genuine
feeling, penetrate deep into the subconscious mind. Use words
that convey emotion, such as beauty, power, love, eager,
cheerful, flowing, happily, and fabulous. When possible, use
the term joy or ease with your affirmations. "I enjoy doing . .
. "or "it is easy for me to . . .."

The goals you have identified in chapter five now need to be worded
into affirmations. Using the above guidelines, draft your
affirmations. For example, if your goal is to improve your memory,
your affirmation would be: "I have an excellent memory. I easily
recall information I have been exposed to."

## Visualization

Visualization is the mental picture of a future goal or event.
Visualization records the goal in the subconscious mind. Believe
the visualization is real. This will cause the goal to be accepted
quickly by your subconscious mind. The more realistic the
visualization, the more effective it will be. Have faith and believe
that what you visualize will occur. Once it is in the subconscious
mind, it activates your Creative Power. Your mind thinks with
pictures. What you picture—good or bad-will ultimately be
brought into reality. People who are aware of this "cause and effect
relationship" know that whatever image they hold in their mind
will eventually be produced in their lives.

Picture exactly what you want when you visualize. Know the end
result distinctly in your mind. Rely on the subconscious mind to
point the way. You don't need to know every minute step to your
goal, instead, picture the end result and let the superconscious
show you the way. When you have properly programmed your
goal in the mind, it will find solutions to achieve it.

Creating pictures and visualizing clear images challenge people who are more conceptual than visual. They visualize by holding ideas and feelings about a goal, rather than seeing a clear picture. If you are one of them, all you have to do is feel the outcome. Your mind will activate the Creative Power and materialize the desired result. It is not necessary for you to visualize with great clarity in order for your vision to become reality. Unclear, fragmented pictures can still activate the subconscious mind.

## Using Visualization To Improve Performance

When you are faced with personal challenges, visualize yourself performing with excellence. If you are in a situation where you will be interviewing for a new job, giving a speech, or other performance, familiarize yourself with the surroundings. If possible, visit the location ahead of time and picture yourself achieving perfection. This allows you to mentally practice, and will improve your performance. It gives you the confidence to perform at your best. When it is time to act, you have already successfully done it many times before.

## Visualization Research

In the early 1950's, psychologist Alan Richardson conducted a study at Ohio State University. He randomly picked three groups of students. The first group was instructed to shoot basketball foul shots every day for 20 minutes. The second group was instructed to visualize shooting foul shots daily for 20 minutes. The third group did not practice. Several weeks later, they re-evaluated the participants. The first group that practiced shooting daily improved by 24 percent. The group that mentally practiced shooting foul shots improved by 23 percent. The last group, which did not practice, did not improve.

This study is significant, because it reinforces the idea that the mind cannot tell the difference between an actual event and one vividly imagined. Many Olympic and world-class athletes are aware of this principle. They use visualization to improve their performances.

## Visualization Guidelines

- The subconscious will respond better to pictures that are large, clearly focused, bright, and active. Whatever you want, visualize having it. If it is a new house, picture the house exactly as you want it. In your mind's eye, visualize walking from room to room, seeing the furniture, and looking out the windows. See the house as detailed as you can.

- Permanent change occurs from the inside out. When you change the inner picture, your subconscious will produce the drive and energy to manifest your goal into reality. Visualize the new: you will become dissatisfied with the old. It is that dissatisfaction which motivates you to change. This will cause your system to be out of order, which will activate the creative energy and drive to bring your goal into reality.

- The Creative Power is activated when there is a clear picture of the outcome. Picture your destiny by visualizing the end result. See yourself achieving great accomplishments, and having what you want. Visualize what you want, not what you want to avoid.

- Visualize the situation as though you were actually performing the event. If you want a new car, visualize yourself driving it. Visualize and imagine the event in the same way you would experience it. See it from your eyes, looking out.

- Visualize using as many senses as possible. Again, if it is a new car, smell the new car odor, and visualize feeling the seats. Experience the pride of showing it to your family and friends.

Identify the sensory feelings you will experience when the goal is achieved. Sensory feelings include sight, sound, touch, taste, and smell.

## Emotion

Visualization is more effective when you experience emotion with the picture in your mind while you are reciting the affirmation. Emotion energizes the recording in the subconscious. When you combine the words, pictures, and emotion, the affirmation will be accepted and recorded into the subconscious mind faster.

## Imprinting Guidelines

- Imprinting should be done while you are in a relaxed state. Get comfortable, relax, and close your eyes. The best time to imprint goals is when you wake up or before going to sleep. During these times, you are the most relaxed and the subconscious is most susceptible to suggestion.

- If a negative image exists in the mind, the subconscious must release it. Acknowledge the negative image and expel it. Affirm that your subconscious mind is now able to accept the new belief. Use visualization to erase or cancel the idea from your mind.

- Affirmations need to be realistic and said with belief and genuine feeling. When you first set your goal, there is a good chance you will think of it as a dream, not knowing for sure if you will succeed. Act as though the affirmation is true. With repetition and time, the affirmation will be accepted by your subconscious mind. You must inwardly know you will achieve the goal. All doubt must be eliminated from your mind. When this occurs, you will start working toward achieving the goal.

- Mentally think of the affirmation, bring in feelings of emotion, and picture the goal complete. Do this for approximately 30 seconds and relax, letting the picture fade. Clear your mind and repeat the process, programming the goal a second time. Do this for each of your goals. Some goals will require several affirmations. For example, with athletics, you may want to improve several areas of your game. It should take you ten minutes to program six to eight goals.

- Imagine your goal frequently. The amount of time you spend thinking about your goal is an indication of how much you want it. Throughout the day, repeat it to yourself as often as you can, whenever you have spare time. Affirmations should be repeated five to 20 times daily.

- Don't overwork the subconscious mind by affirming too many things at once. Concentrate on one or two areas of your life and make several related affirmations for change. This will make it easier to remember the affirmations. If you affirm too many concepts, what happens is similar to what happens when you are given many projects and asked to do them all at once. It is often harder to work on multiple projects than to concentrate on completing one.

- When you are changing a habit, and you find yourself slipping back into your old ways, be easy on yourself. Catch yourself and affirm, "That is not like me, the next time I will . . ." then picture the successful new attribute.

- Don't talk about the affirmation with other people; they will notice on their own.

- At some point you will recognize there is no longer a need to continue saying the affirmation. This will naturally occur after saying it for one to three months. You will know the affirmation has become reality and the changes have been made.

- Mentally thank the Creative Power for all the good that has been brought into your life.

- You will notice a change in your belief as you imprint your goals. You might have started with a vague desire for a goal, but by using proper imprinting techniques, your desire will grow stronger. When the goal is properly imprinted, it will feel as if it is part of you, and it will become a burning desire. You will be constantly thinking about it, and your reticular activating system will be alert to let in information that is helpful. The change is working naturally from the inside out. You will be obsessed with desire to complete the goal. You will think about it all the time and work relentlessly toward achieving it.

## Imprinting Exercise

Imagine you are in your kitchen, standing in front of the cutting board. You take a lemon and, using a sharp knife, cut a lemon wedge. The wedge is extremely juicy. You take it and squeeze it in your mouth.

What did you experience? Did you react as though the lemon was real? Did you taste the tartness? Did your body react to the visualization and produce saliva?

You just felt what it is like to imprint a goal using vivid imagination. The subconscious cannot distinguish the difference between a real event and a vividly imagined experience, felt with emotion.

## *Summary*

- The subconscious mind can be programmed.
- To effect lasting personal change, affirm and visualize with feeling.
- Thank the Creative Power for all that is working in your life.
- Affirm great things, and the power within will respond. What you believe with conviction, you will achieve.

# CONQUERING OBSTACLES AND FEAR

Problems are messages from the universe. The all-knowing Higher Power knows the lessons you need to learn and gives you those learning experiences. Examine your problems and try to find the hidden message or lesson. Many people discover things about themselves that could not be learned any other way. When you reflect back on life, obstacles encountered are often viewed as life's most important experiences.

There will be times when you will face challenges that will seem insurmountable. View them as temporary setbacks, as teaching experiences, and learn from them. Know life is constantly changing, and challenging times never last. Never think of yourself as a failure and never let obstacles stop you from your goal. Successful people encounter obstacles, deal with them, and stay focused on their life plan. People without a plan are easily distracted and find it difficult to stay the course. Most people succeed when confronted with crisis. They do this by handling the situation as best they can.

> *I never had a policy; I have just tried to do my very best each and every day.*
>
> ABRAHAM LINCOLN
> (SIXTEENTH PRESIDENT OF THE UNITED STATES 1809-1865)

Problems need to be confronted when they are detected. It is better to confront them early and manage them while they are small, rather than waiting for them to drain your mental energy and become catastrophic. You have the power to defeat any obstacle. When challenges occur, rely on your inner consciousness to provide the answers. The Higher Power knows the direction in which you need to be going.

> *A life not put to the test is not worth living.*
> EPICTETUS (PHILOSOPHER 50-120)

## Negative Emotions

Negative emotions, such as hate, worry, regret, remorse, resentment, hostility, envy, and jealousy are destructive. They impede the creative process and block the Higher Power. Your emotions must align with this power to keep it within you. To have happiness and peace of mind, you must be free of negative emotions.

> *Holding on to anger is like grasping a hot coal with the intent of throwing it at someone else; you are the one who gets burned.*
> BUDDHA (568-488 BC)

## Forgiveness

Forgive anyone who has harmed you. Do this for your benefit, not theirs. Harboring resentment and hate will waste energy and take power from you. You will be unable to get what you want, as long as you harbor anger and fail to forgive. Forgiveness changes your focus of thought. Replacing negative, destructive emotions with positive, constructive emotions will bring goodness into your life. This allows you to use life's energy to pursue your goals. Life is easier with positive emotions. Always think positive, constructive thoughts. This is a secret to happiness and peace of mind.

> *To be wronged is nothing unless you continue to remember it.*
> CONFUCIUS (CHINESE PHILOSOPHER 551-479 BC)

## Fear

Fear is a negative thought. Most fear is learned, and comes from worrying about something that might happen in the future. Nearly all fear fails to materialize. Your imagination usually overestimates and distorts what you expect will happen. In order to grow, you have to confront your fears.

The more you are required to give up, the greater the fear, in most cases. The more attached you are to your present self-image, the more fear you will face when you encounter growth opportunities. In order to grow and fulfill your life's purpose, you will have to change your life. You will have to give up some things, in order to get others.

## Getting What You Want Involves Fear

When you try to fulfill your life's purpose, you will feel fear. Fulfilling your life's purpose will require you to grow. Fear always accompanies growth. Feeling fear is a signal that you have selected a purpose which will make you stretch. In fact, if you don't feel fear, that is a sign you are not stretching enough. Feel the fear, and know it is part of the change process. It is there for everyone. We all face it, and we all must conquer it. When you move through fear, it will turn into an adventure.

Whatever you want, ask yourself, "What is the most harmful thing that can happen if things don't work out as planned?" Identify what that is, then imagine dealing with the issue. If you can handle it, proceed with your quest. Be sure to imagine living your life without accomplishing your goal or life's purpose. Is this the life you want to live?

Be willing to take chances in life. Facing your fears requires courage. Courage is taking action in spite of the fear. You can face life's challenges with anxiety and doubt, or bravery and self-confidence.

Face your fears! It is better to face them and fail, then to cower and fail to try. When you fail to try, you have really experienced failure!

## How To Conquer Fear

You have the power to conquer fear. The quickest way to eliminate fear, is to have faith in your ability to defeat it. The subconscious mind can be programmed to replace fear with faith and courage. The ultimate goal is to remove fear from your life and replace it with faith, followed by action that will allow you to overcome. This will result in experience and knowledge that can be used to conquer future fear.

> *Do the thing you are afraid to do, and the death of fear is certain.*
> RALPH WALDO EMERSON (AMERICAN POET/ESSAYIST 1803-1882)

## Ways To Conquer Fear

- Define the fear you will face.
- Concentrate on what you want, rather than what you fear.
- Change your attitude. View your fear as an adventure.
- Prepare for the future event. Learn all you can, prior to attempting what it is that you want.
- Start small: scale down what you want to do by practicing it in a reduced-risk environment.
- Acknowledge the fear and proceed cautiously. The way to conquer fear is to face your fear head on and go through it.
- Celebrate success! Reward yourself as you make incremental strides toward your goal.

## Risk

We must constantly choose between the path of safety and the path of growth. There is nothing wrong with choosing the safe path, as long as it fulfills you. However, by always choosing the safe road, your life can become routine and boring. When you sense that this is occurring, it is time to take some risk. Listen to your inner voice. If your life is miserable, listen and start taking action to make it better. Dare to fulfill your inner desire. Go for it!

It is important to consult your inner voice for guidance prior to confronting your fear. Confronting your fear requires you to face your fear head on and move through it. As you move through your fear, you will encounter a point of no return. At the point of no return, you will need to press forward, knowing the risk. This requires full commitment and concentration.

> *We must walk consciously only part way toward our goal, and then leap in the dark to our success.*
> HENRY DAVID THOREAU (AMERICAN ESSAYIST 1817-1862)

When you are working toward the future, you will experience a sense of growth. Give up looking for security and start looking for opportunities to grow. When you do this, your life will have meaning. Growing involves risk. Successful risk-taking adds excitement to life.

> *A ship in harbor is safe, but that is not what ships are built for.*
> JOHN SHEDD

## Summary
- The Universe sends you problems that consist of lessons you need to learn.
- Negative thoughts poison the mind and cause disharmony in your body.
- Eliminate all negative emotions from your life. Forgive others who have harmed you, so your mind can be free of negative energy.
- To get what you want will require you to grow and face your fears. As you grow, consult your inner voice for guidance.
- Change fear into adventure.

# CONCLUSION

You now know the principles that can change your life. The subconscious mind, through the power of thought, will bring you what you want. Imagine life as you want it. Form a picture of the desired end result in your mind. The power within will act on your picture, and manifest your goals in your life. Focus your energy towards this purpose and you will record a new, dominant image within the subconscious mind. Your mind will activate the drive and desire to bring the changes about. Your thoughts are powerful; they have brought you to where you are in life today. This is equally true for those who are successful and those who are troubled.

---

**When The Following Elements Are Present, You Are Unstoppable:**

✔ You believe in your goal and expect it to manifest.
✔ You have faith, commitment, and resolve to accomplish your objective.
✔ The subconscious has been imprinted with your wants.

---

Few people have a good understanding of the principles outlined in this book. The fact that you have read it will make you much wiser. The laws are impersonal; they work for everyone. Your thoughts are creative; control them. The desire you have in your heart, and the vision you hold in your mind, will determine your destiny. Keep your thoughts positive and never picture failure. You will attract the feeling you give out. Like begets like, and what you believe, you will become. Use this information wisely, for the principles that are used to create can also destroy.

When you decide what it is that you want, stay focused on where you are going. Be willing to pay the price in terms of time, energy, and desire. Life's riches will be handed to you. The process of achievement will evolve with time. Move slowly and steadily: work a little every day on that which will move you closer to achieving your goal. When the farmer plants a crop, he must work hand and hand with the creator to bring it to harvest. So it is with your wants. The power within is extremely efficient in accomplishing the end result.

Your inner wants are really needs. Don't postpone those desires. They come from your basic nature and are clues to what you can become. You have one ride on this earth and you would be wise to make the most of it. To settle for less would be a mistake.

> *Twenty years from now, you will be more disappointed by the things you didn't do than by the ones you did. So throw off the bowlines, sail away from the safe harbor: Catch the trade winds in your sails. Explore. Dream.*
> MARK TWAIN (AMERICAN AUTHOR 1835-1910)

In closing, I am honored you have chosen this book to enrich your life. I wish you happiness and prosperity. Use these principles to make the world a better place. Be sure your thoughts bring goodness to benefit others. Thank God for his help along the way.

> *Happiness does not consist in having what you want, but wanting what you have.*
> CONFUCIUS (CHINESE PHILOSOPHER 551-479 BC)

# *INDEX*

# ABOUT THE AUTHOR

Twenty years ago John Brinsmead became aware that there were life changing principles that were not taught in school. He started reading everything he could find dealing with success and success principles. Before long John had read or listened to 600+ books and books on tape. He started applying the principles to his own life and discovered that they worked amazingly well.

    With retirement on the horizon John was unsure of what he wanted to do in the next phase of his life. He used the principles and exercises that are in this book to analyze his life. He was able to identify his dream. That was the start of a journey that resulted in the book you are holding in your hands. It took twenty years to research and six years to write. John used the principles in the book to create the book. The system worked for him and it can work for you!

    John has worked as a police officer, investigator, and a public administrator for the last 30 years. He has a Bachelor degree in Public Administration, a Master's degree in Business Administration, and he is a Certified Fraud Examiner.

# Easy Order Form

**Email orders:** http://JohnBrinsmead.com
**Telephone orders:** 800-499-5061
**Postal Orders:** Mirrormont Press, PO Box 3466, Renton, WA 98056

Name: _____

Address: _____

_____

City: _____ State: _____ Zip: _____

Telephone: _____

Email Address: _____

| QTY | | | |
|---|---|---|---|
| | FINDING YOUR DESTINY | X $15.95 | |
| | Sales Tax: Please add 8.4% for products shipped to Washington addresses. | | |
| | Shipping: US Ground: $4 for the first book and $2 for each additional book. | | |
| | International Air: $9 for first book and $5 for each additional book. | | |
| | Total | | |

**Payment:**
Check      Money Order
Credit Card:  Visa    MC    AMEX    DISCOVER

Card Number: _____

Name on the card: _____

Exp. Date: _____